For the Epsteins,

Our friend John's
unfortunate problem has brought
you and me together. You are
superior in your own lives —
César isn't our only hero.
Each of us in our own ways
strives for a better world.

Susan
3/3/99

I laughed, I cried. I remembered. Susan's moving and exquisitely crafted poetry brings to life the men, women and children who toil long hours, under the most difficult conditions, to bring the fruits of the earth to our tables.

—ROSEMARY MATSON, award-winning humanitarian and global activist; co-founder with her husband, The Reverend Howard Matson, of The Unitarian Universalist Migrant Ministry

This is an unforgettable portrait of César Chávez and his union during thirty turbulent years of recent history.

—ANNE LOFTIS, author of *Witnesses to the Struggle: Imaging the 1930s California Labor Movement*

Under Drake's skillful hands, César Chávez achieves a fascinating third dimension, rounding out the icon most of us only knew from newspaper reports.

—MAUDE MEEHAN, poet, *Washing the Stones, Chipping Bone* and national poetry anthologies

...great story-telling. History in verse...reads like a novel.

—PHILIP J. WAGNER, poet, National Writers Union

Susan Drake's poetic eye captures... intimate and disarming still-frames from the life of César Chávez... a flawed hero.

—MARK R. DAY, journalist, film maker, author of *Forty Acres: César Chávez and the Farmworkers*

What emerged for me in reading *Fields of Courage* is heart. Big heart, brave heart, grieving heart, cheering heart, and, ultimately, accepting heart.

—DON MARSH, widely-published poet and novelist: *An Ice Cream Communion* and *The Stone Humpers*

Here's César's imprint on Susan's vulnerable, liberal conscience told through the most enduring literary form: the love poem.

—FRANK BARDACKE, author of the forthcoming *Beneath the California Sun: Farm Workers, César Chávez and the UFW*

FIELDS OF COURAGE

FIELDS OF COURAGE

Remembering César Chávez
&
the People Whose Labor Feeds Us

SUSAN SAMUELS DRAKE

MANY NAMES PRESS
SANTA CRUZ, CALIFORNIA

Photographs are used with permission of the photographers:

César 1966, César with Garcia and Boyle 1980 © 1998 Susan Samuels Drake

Untitled, Thirsty for Care, Cucumber Harvesters © 1975 Matthew Drake

César and Juana 1982 © 1982 Victor Aleman

Senator Robert Kennedy © 1966 Jon Lewis

Portrait 1969, César and Juana Estrada Chávez © 1975 Bob Fitch

Carolina Vasquez 1966, Breaking the 26-day Fast 1968, Señor Zapata,
A Sense of Justice © 1970 John A. Kouns

Sí, Chávez! No, Wilson! cartoon © 1994 Paul Duginski,
used with permission of the artist.

The poem *Unskilled?* appeared in the 1998 Cabrillo College *Porter Gulch Review*.

"La Victoria" quotation from Mahatma Gandhi: César Chávez,
El Malcriado, April, 1970

Cover painting *Watsonville Strawberry Workers*
© 1998 Harry Federico, used with permission of the artist.
Book and cover design copyright © 1998 Kate Hitt
Cover composite: Graciela Hernandez

Title page line drawing © 1998 Bob Samuels, used with permission of the artist.

Type and b/w composition: Annie Browning / talking circles

ISBN 0-9652575-6-8
Library of Congress Catalogue Card Number 98-68606

Printed and published in the United States of America by Kate Hitt
at Many Names Press.   www.manynamespress.com

First Edition

This book is dedicated
to the people
who plant, nurture and harvest,
especially
you brave ones
who persist
with nonviolence
to make your place in the sun
a healthy, safe and
economically viable one.

You inspire me.

table of contents

list of illustrations

photo section one
César Chávez 1966
Thirsty for Care
Untitled 1975
Cucumber Harvesters 1975

photo section two
Carolina Vasquez 1966
Senator Robert Kennedy
Breaking the 26-day Fast
Portrait of César 1969

photo section three
César and Juana Estrada Chávez, 1975
Señor Zapata
Tom, Susan, Matthew and Jim Drake
A Sense of Justice

photo section four
Movement's 20th Anniversary, 1982
César, Boyle and Garcia, circa 1980
César and his mother, Juana
Sí, Chávez! No, Wilson! cartoon, 1994

acknowledgments

To Jim Drake, my husband during the 1960s and 1970s and the farm workers' man of many roles, thank you for ushering me into a new way of looking at life.

To Chris Hartmire, boss, friend and counselor, thank you for your patience.

Muchísimas gracias to Jessie Ortega, Esther Rodríguez, the Tony Gonzales and the Gonzales who lived behind us in Goshen, the Guajardo-Arispes, and to Sebastián Zamora—your examples as farm laborers prepared me to participate in one of our country's momentous turning points.

With the open-heartedness of Helen Chávez, then César Chávez and Dolores Huerta, I found ways to help further their dreams. I am grateful that they also helped reshape my thinking.

To poet Maude Meehan, *abrazos.* Your exemplary vulnerability and love of the craft continue to help me convert feelings into poetry.

My brother Bob Samuels added a new dimension to our tie: his newly discovered artful line drawing enhances my writing. I am incapable of expressing how deeply his collaboration touches me.

The visual images of *La Causa* enrich the portrait I render in words. Harry Federico sees beauty in the way workers connect with the land; his watercolor is on the cover. Photographers Victor Aleman, Matt Drake, Bob Fitch, John Kouns and Jon Lewis take us into the soul of César and the movement. Paul Duginski's political cartoon combines the best of graphics, heart and message. Each artist sacrificed financial gain in order to share in this book. It is an honor to showcase their work.

Printer, editor and publisher Kate Hitt of Many Names Press, cover designer Graciela Hernandez, typophile Annie Browning and copy editor Rita Townsend are new friends whose technical skills, encouragement, and parallel focus brought my dream to fruition. They helped make this book feel like a gift, not a job.

To numerous friends who kibitzed and kept my spirits intact, especially during my busy or grouchy days, thank you. The list is too long to print, but you know who you are.

Susan Samuels Drake
Soquel, California

p r o l o g u e

Letter to my family

IN 1962, around the time of his 35th birthday on March 31st, César Chávez began going door to door in farm worker communities to see if there was interest in developing an association that would help resolve unjust working and living conditions. Six weeks later, César began training my husband, Jim, to become a community organizer.

On May 14th of that year, I wrote my parents and two brothers in Atherton, California, patronizing words that show how much I had to learn. Written from Goshen, California, in the Central Valley between Fresno and Bakersfield on Highway 99:

"*Jim's going to work with a little Mexican man...*"

No point mentioning the man's name—who ever heard of César Chávez? A week later, my husband wrote to my family:

For the past week, and it will continue, I have been traveling around with Caesar [sic] Chávez who has been a top 'executive' in the Community Service Organization. Primarily it is a Mexican-American group which concentrates on one community at a time, organizes the minority races, and strikes out against one particular problem at a time; for instance, need of water, sewage, police protection, or police brutality... Caesar is trying to take a census of the farm workers in the San Joaquin, getting them registered [to vote] and trying to get a feeling for their grievances. They are pretty out of sorts with the AWOC (AFL-CIO branch of Agricultural Workers Union). The unions have not gone directly to the people to gain support for their strikes and have had nothing but bitter experiences in trying to orga-nize the farm workers. Caesar is interested in some alternative to the Labor Union, perhaps a Farm Workers Association which would act as a cooperative and would bargain directly with the rancher (always with the threat of a strike as a weapon, but not unless really needed). Caesar is much more interested in having a united body which can go to work in Sacramento to change legislation rather than a strike here and there. What we have been doing (really, I am not doing anything, I just go along and observe and try to stay 'neutral' which is really impossible) is to have house meetings with Mexican-Americans, Filipinos, and Negroes in an effort to have teams go out and do the registering... and in the process to discover the grass-roots leaders. I have been in a number of such meetings as well as in some of the liveliest bars and in one week have learned more than in seven years of school! Caesar takes me with him EVERYWHERE and it is just like having a ticket into the very hearts of the poor.

He is a man of great compassion, ...a farm laborer himself, and yet one who has educated <u>himself</u>... (only went to 7th grade). His reading habits... from Aristotle to the Cobey Report on Farm Labor.

Love,

Jim

introduction

"I HAVE NEVER LOVED nor hated anyone as much as I love and hate César Chávez," I used to say to friends during the years when I was the farm labor leader's secretary. Loved, because César was bigger than anyone I'd ever known—big in spirit, physical endurance, smarts, generosity and charm. Hated? Simply a distortion of my immense frustration. I was young, and when our interactions felt too much like those I had with my father, I took all César's short-tempered words personally as I did with Dad. Such is the stuff of families, and César created a kind of family which I walked into in 1962. My life in that family changed me, as it changed the face of California agriculture and as it changed forever—if not the way farm workers are treated—the way they are able to see themselves.

Shortly after César died in 1993, a strong supporter of the farm workers' movement fumed, "I'll never forgive him for how he treated some of the staff." I wondered, since I'd finally digested and let go of my own anger toward César, if I could help her and others see the César I knew. I resumed work on the manuscript, at that point already a decade in the writing, about my experience. When I first told César I was writing, he laughed and with his usual clever come-back, announced, "Okay, then I get to write one about you."

I knew César 31 years and only one other person I knew of, who knew César as long as I did, has written a book about him. The Chávez I knew was mightily gifted but certainly not without normal feelings and reactions to pressure—and the pressure was enormous.

So who was César Estrada Chávez? Certainly, no single word or phrase or book can contain him. His titles were many: organizer, prophet of sustainable development, eager recycler (he even saved vegetable seeds from his garden to plant year after year), health nut, student of dozens of subjects. He was a powerful, persuasive speaker, labor leader, charismatic hero; American-born farm worker of Mexican descent; the Mexican Martin Luther King; America's Gandhi.

Friend and foe alike admit that no one accomplished what César did. No one else inspired 100,000 farm workers to shed their independent ways and sign up for membership in a fledgling labor union. No one else used nonviolence so effectively as an organizing principle; only a handful of others had even tried to, in the 1930s. César integrated people from diverse cultural backgrounds into a movement that swept its way into political, medical, legal, economic, environmentalist and religious circles.

What was the scene in agriculture that caused César to crave change? First, the term "farm workers" refers only to the people who plant, cultivate, irrigate and harvest. It does not include supervisors or management in agribusiness. Concerning injustice, the poems tell the story on many fronts: wages, on-the-job safety, health care, housing and education. Retirement wasn't even in the *campesino's* vocabulary. In every arena farm workers were—and are—expected to endure devastating conditions—never coming close to the quality of life that mainstream, industrialized or white-collar Americans had come to expect. Politicians backed agribusiness, as they still do, to keep the quality of life for farm laborers substandard.

Prior to becoming the United Farm Workers, AFL-CIO, the fledgling National Farm Workers Association had two successes that seeded the untimely, now famous Grape Strike of 1965: a rent strike at a Tulare County-owned labor camp, and, in cooperation with many other organizations, the good riddance of the *bracero* program. *Braceros* were Mexicans brought into this country with the blessing of the United States government to work for less money than the American workers earned. (Beware the reintroduction of this program under the euphemistically titled Guest Worker Program).

Early in the 1970s, by rallying farm workers, legislators and consumers, César signed nearly 100 contracts covering workers in table and wine grapes, lettuce, citrus, and later mushrooms in California, Arizona and Florida. On many ranches, wages rose and pesticide applications were regulated. Growers were required to have portable toilets and drinkable water on-site during work hours. Through the efforts of César and others, the back-breaking short-handled hoe was outlawed in California. Although the effectiveness of the California Agricultural Labor Relations Act depends on whether the sitting governor favors workers or growers, the Act, when carried out, sets the table for fairness. The Act permits farm workers to hold elections in order to choose union representation. Most farm workers in California benefited from the union's successes, whether those workers were covered by a UFW contract or not.

Dues-paying members of the UFW, AFL-CIO working under union contract enjoyed added benefits: collective bargaining, grievance resolution, medical coverage, and a pension plan. Labor contractors, often called *coyotes* (for the scurrilous reputation that accompanied the unsafe and/or greedy ways they provided workers for the ranches), were replaced by the union's hiring hall.

But in 1973, when the first negotiated contracts began to expire, attempts to renew them failed. Growers and union staff were unfamiliar with dealing respectfully with one another at a bargaining table. With financial resources far greater than those of the UFW, growers gathered all the anti-union politicians and lawyers they could muster. Even when the AFL-CIO stepped in with financial contributions, the combined funds were no match for agribusiness' corporate dollars. For years, the Teamsters Union signed "sweetheart" agreements with the growers to undermine the UFW efforts, the Teamos (Teamsters) promising not to press for the changes in working conditions that the UFW championed.

Another stumbling block to progress formed within the UFW administration itself. The burgeoning union was staffed by people inexperienced in operating a farm labor union. After all, there was no pattern to follow: this was and is the first enduring union for agricultural workers. The Teamsters include members who perform agriculturally-related work; but, unlike UFW, the people who work with the crops are not the Teamsters' only or even primary focus.

The UFW was left to convince discouraged workers that their union dues would still be judiciously spent. Growers, legislators, union staff and competing unions were to blame for ineffective contract enforcement and the breakdown of negotiations. Agribusiness had won.

As the end of the 20th century nears, current situations involving farm workers remind me of the years before the UFW. Work-related injuries remain extraordinarily high among farm laborers. Workers still earn sub-standard wages, often below the minimum wage. Farm workers' children find school difficult for a number of reasons: some stay home and babysit so parents can work, some lack transportation to school, and often parents' limited education hinders their ability to assist with homework. In some states, including California, law forbids teaching general subjects to non-English-speaking children in their native language; this delays the learning process for some children. Other laws put farm workers at further disadvantage in the areas of housing, social services, and medical services. A very small percentage of the nation's farm workers are covered by labor contracts, as of this writing.

What are the obstacles to a better life for farm workers? Once one's union membership is known, the threat of being fired or not being rehired is probable. Justice in the fields is even harder to achieve now that agribusiness is more sophisticated in protecting its interests. Corporations structure themselves to skirt the California Agricultural Labor Relations Act (ALRA). In at least one case, the company says it only ships produce without actually owning land. But that corporation's board members own large landholdings and employ hundreds of workers. Small farms do exist, but the big-business mentality persists since often these growers would not survive without using the corporate storage and shipping facilities. Sadly, many who hold smaller acreage are former farm workers who form new alliances to management rather than to their brothers and sisters in the fields. For union members, violence is still a big threat, either at the hand of anti-union co-workers or law enforcement officers with strong agribusiness sympathies.

"We are humans with feelings. We are not criminals," a Mexican lettuce worker in Salinas said recently, when the cops beat UFW members where she works. Her lips quivered with pride and would not let loose her flood of tears in front of the meeting of mostly-Anglo UFW supporters. She and her husband said they could not understand why more than a decade had passed, yet their employer failed to negotiate the contract required by the ALRA when the workers at that ranch had won an election for UFW representation.

As long as farm workers face this kind of disrespect, they will need leadership that is as determined, persevering, and intelligent as César Chávez offered. They will need fair and effective negotiators. They will need to work together, not splinter into several unions. They will need a public that grasps the seriousness of their age-old struggle. The concept that workers and growers are interdependent is almost fatally impaired by the historic obstacle of unsympathetic, uncooperative Haves employing Have-nots.

Today, most companies growing produce are hell-bent on keeping this union out of the fields. What keeps them from negotiating with their employees? Economics? Fear of what several thousand unified workers might expect? Why aren't the bosses concerned as farm workers and consumers are about pesticide damage to our health and that of the earth? Why is it taking so long to train workers about methods for decreasing the rate of on-the-job injuries?

Before you read about the man who dared to think he could help answer those questions, could change working conditions for farm workers, I wish to share two opinions of my work. A young Latina said to me, "Some of us don't want to see César more human; some of what you write here is hard to take." Someone else the day before told me, "After reading your poems, I see César's humanness now and I actually like him even more."

History must deal with how much of our heroes' imperfections we record and how much we erase. I write of the light and shadows of the man to remind us that "charismatic" and "saintly" are expensive words. People around the world use those adjectives when talking of the former farm worker. Yet how many understand the price César, his wife Helen, and their children paid for his resolute leadership? Surely knowing more about our past leaders can teach us how to raise, discover, or train leaders for the present and the future (and maybe forgive them their trespasses).

Although some people hold onto their resentments regarding César, any time I hear someone venting hostilities about him, I'm apt to interrupt with, "No one else brought about the improvements that César did." The response is always a resounding, "Absolutely."

César died on April 23, 1993 in Arizona, not far from his Yuma birthplace. His legacy, felt most strongly in the farm labor union movement and among Mexican-Americans and Mexicans, is also felt at a deeply personal level by millions who knew, met or only read about him. From him, we learned that the victim stance serves no one well. The *Sí se puede*—Yes, it can be done— attitude, planted by a small-statured man with big ideas, is the inheritance that must see us through yet another round in the battle for human dignity and decency.

Once, during a UFW staff party, César and I were dancing. In the midst of the gaiety, his eyes took on an imploring puppy look and he asked, "Why do you like me?" The question caught me completely off-guard. I gave him some vapid answer; I let him down that night. Now I realize he always trusted my honest, even blunt or tactless, answers. I suppose, beneath the cloak of power, lay that haunting need we all have, that need to know why we matter. Maybe now I can answer César's question better.

CÉSAR

1966

© *Susan Samuels Drake*

THIRSTY FOR CARE

© *Matthew Drake*

U N T I T L E D

1975

© *Matthew Drake*

CUCUMBER HARVESTERS

1975

© *Matthew Drake*

IN THE FIELDS

Capital is only the fruit of labor and could never have existed if labor had not first existed. Labor is the superior of capital, and deserves much higher consideration.

—Abraham Lincoln
Message to Congress, 1861

PORTRAIT—1962
California Migrant Ministry Staff Retreat

The meeting breaks
we reshuffle chairs
so the man in the corner can join our circle
of shiny-faced innocents
eager to eradicate exploitation
in California's agricultural fields.

That man in the corner
dark
dark sweater
dark skin
quiet as dawn.
That man in the corner
lights up the room
with fresh, bold ideas
about tapping into farm workers' natural
resources, giving them
courage to speak up
for themselves.

His name is César Chávez.
He pronounces his name
so do we
Ceez-ur
but years
many years later
when Latinos stand prouder
because of him
they pronounce it Cess-ar
the way it was meant to be.

WHERE WE CAME FROM

How hard
for César's proud parents to abandon their store
the forty acres around it near Yuma
and hit the dusty trail
with hundreds and hundreds of out-of-work Americans.
In the big scheme
their suffering
and his
helped thousands of other farm workers
believe when he said things like,
I know the work is hard
very hard
I know we deserve respect.
You work all day
deserve to go home at night
with enough money in your pocket
enough dignity
to continue.

Most farm workers lived in broken houses, in tents, in cars
not like that warm old adobe
where César was born in Arizona's Gila Valley.
In 1933, a land-hungry neighbor
swooped down on family farm crippled by crop-failure.
Tax money couldn't be raised:
the neighbor-banker denied César's Papa application
for a loan that might have saved the Chávez place.

Librado drove the five children and wife Juana
up through the oven-like temperatures of Brawley,
over to California's cooler coast—Ventura and Half Moon Bay.
The family landed in San Jose
on César's mother's birthday, June 24, 1939.
It was just a day before my first birthday
but he was already 12.

The Chávez house in San Jose sat
in *el barrio*
called *Sal Si Puedes*—Get Out If You Can.
Mine, twenty miles away, was in another enclave
called Palo Alto
which might as well have been called
Get In If You Can Afford To.

I trusted everybody.
César trusted few.
The store keepers gave me free candy.
They cheated him and his little brother Richard.
If my toys had been stolen,
as theirs were,
my Daddy the lawyer
would have gone to the police and gotten them back.
But already the police were not César's family's friends.
And because someone swindled César's father
the son's determination grew
subtly strong as old grape vines
to educate fellow *campesinos*
so people would not take advantage of them.

Even though César quit school to work
his teachers didn't quit him.
Sister Rita, Uncle Ramon, his mother and grandmother
taught César the history of his *gente*, his people—
how Grandpa Césario had been a slave in Mexico until
he escaped in 1880 and came to Texas.

César was 25 when
someone showed him a way out of the *barrio*.
Fred Ross—
a nice name that made the cocky *pachuco* suspicious—
probably just another social worker.

In a Chávez living room meeting
Fred spoke
about changing things and
not waiting for someone else to do it.
Fred won César over
with earnest, practical, no bull-shitness.

Ten years later
when I was 24
I met my ticket out of affluent innocence
when I met César.

In a few ways we were not so different.
Both our Dads drove Studebakers and called us nicknames.
César's *pachuco* garb of the 1950s no longer defined him
any more than my cashmere and pearls did me.
We rode out of our respective status quos
where we'd caged crusader instincts
because our friends didn't think crusading was cool.
Still, our meeting was unlikely.
It was even more unlikely
that we would weave our lives so tightly together.

AND THE MEEK SHALL INHERIT

When I stepped from Daddy's world of suits
into the land of dirt-smudged, grape-juiced, cotton-fuzzed jeans,
doors opened easily in farm worker homes
yet my white skin didn't fit.
I declined to accept the proffered tamale—
maybe it robbed one of the six little faces standing
mouths open
watching my every cheerful-nervous move.
Yet the brown hand
engraved as any ancient vine by the sun
insisted
with a smile for reinforcement.

When I sat down with my baby son
our hosts haloed us with smiles.
Their sons, before running out to play,
peeked at my little white boy who
soon as he could crawl
studied boyhood at their hands.

Later, wrapped in the scent of aged walls
freshly scrubbed floors
boiling pinto beans
cilantro
I contemplated what it would be like
to   get up every morning at 4 or 5
     make tortillas
     warm up beans
     scramble eggs with *nopales*
     roll them with salsa for burritos
     diaper the babies
     drive them to an older lady's home for watching
     put a dollar's worth of gas into the car
     pray the old Chevie makes it as far as the field

bend like a human paper clip over row crops
for hours beyond an office worker's day
try to ignore the urge to pee in a field with no toilets
stifle thirst if I didn't want to drink from a smelly open bucket
deny throbbing wrists and sore back.

Some days there would be no orchards, no fields
only the smell of the County Hospital emergency room
trying to get answers
    to open wounds,
    to pesticide-laced blood
    to dagger-pain at wrist or spine.

But with their hospitality and patience,
eventually farm workers made me feel all warm
welcome
the way I used to
snuggling my four-year-old self
under the pink satin comforter
on my big-girl bed.

I can dip silver spoons into applesauce
slide freckled pink arms into a cotton t-shirt
sip red wine but
I can't really know
what it's like
to live the back-breaking, spirit-threatening existence
of those whose labor brought me these gifts.

Unskilled?

Anyone
    who has maintained a successful garden
knows
anyone
    who says farm workers are unskilled
lies.

GIVE ME YOUR HUNGRY

From across the Mexican border he comes
in a cast-off school bus
or broken-down truck
that sometimes dumps him in the desert
before he ever sees work.

If he's lucky,
the labor contractor, *el coyote*, takes him
into the lush farm lands of California
of Texas, Arizona, Ohio,
New Jersey, Michigan, Washington, Idaho.

He comes with arms to
plant
pluck
he bends
bends
bends
and reaches
reaches
reaches
for food
he barely has enough money
to buy for himself.

At the end of the day
the contractor's bus takes him far from town
where no one will see
he pays to live in squalor
with the heat—or the wind—
slicing the walls of a labor camp.

Without a car to drive into town for movies,
the *campesino* plays cards,
bets on illegal cockfights,
longs for the hug of his wife
the play-filled squeals of his children.

And, if he's lucky,
the *patrón* won't keep all the money
for the bus ride
for the food
for the bunk.

"ALIENS"

Sun-bleached skulls and torn clothes
toast in that hellish limbo between
international border and job
a smuggling operation gone awry.
It is true today
but even truer
before the University of California
developed machines to replace tomato pickers
before growers disced their crops under and
moved their operations to Mexico.
Before the Immigration and Naturalization Service
tossed wetbacks back
across the American Canal or the Rio Grande into Mexico
in a charade of seriousness
about not having illegal workers in the country.
All the while, the growers paid *los coyotes*
to smuggle the desperate workers
back into the U. S.
over and
over
and over again.
"You don't mess in no strikes
        you work fast
                we don't deport you.
Deal?"

Toxic Shock

Like mammoth steely-grey tarantulas from outer space
crop-dusters drop low,
methodically pace rows of the soon-to-be-lush,
shower our food with poison.
Hard to believe the planes are flown by anyone
with a vision
beyond a paycheck.

Too soon, women and men
return to work in these fields
danger seeping through their skin,
inhaled with each breath
drunk from water buckets left open in the fields or
drawn from underground water tables drowning in pesticides.
What poison rubs off work clothes
onto a snuggled child?
Cancer-cluster towns in farmlands tremor
with wails from mothers of the deformed unborn
and born.

Years before the militant grey copters
the first distant buzz of crop-duster I heard
came from a bi-plane
yellow as corn with red as cherry
against the dusty-blue sky.
As it gained on our ears
quickly we rolled up car windows
my sons held their breath.

Once I recognized the sound
the too-close buzz
looked out my living room window
toward the school
where a bi-plane dusted the field
next to where Matthew and Tommy played at recess.

I called the school secretary: "Find a way
to get that plane out of there."
"Sorry, Mrs. Drake; it's just routine.
It must be safe or
they wouldn't do it."

I hung up
temples pounding time with heart.

If only I could introduce the secretary, the pilot to Sebastian
whose hand cancer erodes a little each day
from a cut that let poison in;
introduce them to husbands whose seed was killed
along with the pests;
to mothers cradling children
bearing unspeakable minuses.

WELFARE

Welfare is the barn
the garage
where agribusiness parks its workers
at the end of the season.

Welfare is the money
our government pays
some of the growers
not to grow
when they don't feel like planting
because the price isn't right.

Growers legislate to keep farm workers
off welfare
and call their own handout
a subsidy.

HISTORY

All those
we picketed
boycotted—
Schenley, DiGiorgio, Giumarra,
United Fruit, Gallo, D'Arrigo, Antle
for starters—
business bullies.
The details of their politics
their financial machinations
too weighty
for me to recall.

Faces
desert-dry crevassed skin
brown eyes struggling for sparkle
flat-line mouths shaping prouder by the year
Faces tell truer history.

part two

IN THE MOVEMENT

*Revolutionary democracy does not require one to
become a saint, only to be self-sacrificing and brave.*

—Frank Bardacke,
activist and writer

THE FORTY ACRES
Headquarters of the National Farm Workers Association
1965

Workers often walked the three miles out of Delano
to The Forty Acres
because they had no car
the bus didn't leave the city limits.

Forty acres
out past the Voice of America
just this side of the dump.
Delano's citizens didn't really notice
when César Chávez came into forty acres of clay
so dense his earth worms spit it out.

One look at these forty acres in the 1960s
a person would have to believe in miracles.
Whirling dust
or miring mud,
flies.
Sun scorched and whittled
the donated Elm and Modesto Ash
to scrawny sticks
because no one watered them regularly
those first weeks their roots clawed the clay.

If someone were going to plant a new Mecca
someone who imagined
a credit union,
a clinic,
offices
and a place for worn-down workers to retire,
a whole complex in adobe and terra cotta
and that someone had no money...

But when César looked into the distance
at impossible dreams
our eyes followed
the visions came true.

WHAT IT MEANS, LA HUELGA

To join a strike means
the stove or car bought on installments
probably both
go back to where they came from.
The union provides
food through a soup kitchen
used clothes trucked up from L.A. and
down from San Francisco supporters
and a very small allowance.
The worker in return transfers all time, hope, pride
to the struggle.

Tedium
carrying picket signs
nibbles away that pride
unless a passerby honks a salute.
More likely the salute is averted eyes
the middle finger.

Established unions may picket a month or two.
Grape strikers
because their union is new
weak
because their bosses are stubborn
walk the line for five years.

WEAPONS FOR THE GRAPE STRIKE

The Growers'
    cropdusters spraying pesticides
    fists
    the press
    the Governor
    the Teamsters' Union
    guns
    goons
    gobs of corporate money

The Farm Worker Movement's
    hope
    patience
    the press
    politicians and entertainers
    legal wizards by the dozens
    global consumer boycott support
    clergy from many faiths
    nonviolence
    El Malcriado to tell the news
    co-operation

PICKETING

I.   The sun yawns and
any hint of chill in the morning air
scoots off as the sun stretches and crawls
up out of the horizon
sending what's left of morning dew
down the leaves
in dusty tear-like streaks.
Picketers walk back and forth at the road's edge near Delano.
At the end of the vineyard,
they double back,
passing one another.
Like red-winged blackbirds
huelga flags fly their bold red-black.

II.   She of the grape strike, *La Huelga*,
bundles her shiny raven hair under a scarf and straw hat,
layers a cotton-tee and a man's cotton, long-sleeved shirt,
shuts out the dust with a bandanna over her nose and mouth.
Polyester slacks send the sun scorching through to her skin.
Cotton trousers would be more comfortable, but
they're hard to find in donations from city folks.
The older women's faces are lined
from years of sun
from the worries of mothers.
Usually docile, once in a while a woman
will plant herself on the side of the road
hands on hips
give a deputy, Teamster or former boss
a piece of her mind.

III.   To the strike-breaking scabs
on the other side of the vineyard's boundaries
strikers shout *"Viva Zapata, Viva Villa"* —
brave men they heard about from their grandparents or
in school
if they found time between working or babysitting.

IV.   If the picket captain calls
over a hand-held, battery-powered megaphone
to workers moving slowly deep in the vineyard,
the grower or his crew foreman
turns his car radio up to ear-breaking screech
on some rock 'n roll station
drowns out the *"Venganse,* come"
and shouts of *"Viva Chávez."*

Many strike-breakers weren't told
they would be replacing their brothers and sisters
who are legal residents of the U.S.
"Huel-ga, huel-ga, huel-ga"
the pickets shout.
But the truth is
any Union supporters left the fields weeks ago.
Those laboring still
are locked in the fields
by fear.

BOYCOTT

"Boycott grapes"
heard in Berkeley classrooms
in New York produce terminals
on the docks in England
and on the floor of Hawaii's legislature.

Many grape pickers couldn't afford
to be philosophical
about justice.
They would not walk out of the vineyards
or risk being seen at union meetings
knowing they were easily
replaced.

So
as if to hold each worker's hand
the public picketed grocers
strangled demand
sent growers begging
for the union label
that courageous eagle.

MARCHING TO SACRAMENTO
March and April 1966

Viva La Huelga and *Viva La Causa* shouts
to let families along the route know
we were coming.

At night the marchers came alive
as if they'd had vitamin B shots
instead of home-cooked beans, rice, tortillas
and extra-special dishes at day's end.
Carolina Vasquez sang
impassioned, mournful, lusty songs.
Some younger pilgrims sprung into vibrant dances—
How, after ten to twelve miles trudging back roads?

Heat, dust, thirst, blisters,
the stuff of pilgrimage days
up the spine of California.
Teenagers and some adults joined in
as if they'd just thought of it.
One woman stood in her front yard
pitcher of water and cups in hand
passing one to each marcher.

César and Helen slept on the sagging sofabed
in our living room a couple of nights.
He accepted Band-Aids, declined Bufferin.
Swollen ankle, blisters, aching back, a fever.
"This is penance, this march."

By the second day, twice as many people marched
as had left Delano.

César turned 39 on that march. And
the Schenley corporation gave him a gift:
recognition of the farm workers' union.
When we heard the news
every cranny of the auditorium filled
with shouts, cat-calls, shrill whistles
and the knowledge we were
on the right track.

El Teatro Campesino
a corps of farm worker-actors
directed by masterminds Luis and Augie
brought nightly messages to spur us on.
In a voice described best as euphonious
with a dash of salsa
Luis read *Plan de Delano*
proclaiming breadth of a movement
encompassing diversity
stridently striving toward an unnamed horizon.

For more than a month
more than three hundred forty miles,
pilgrims trudged the road of determination
joined along the way
by brothers and sisters of the fields
until

Easter morning
last day of the march
many of the *originales* had made it
all the way to Sacramento
melted into swarms of thousands
other farm workers
unionists
consumers
politicians
priests and nuns
and children.
So many,
counters in helicopters
couldn't agree on the number.

Memories stamped in me that day:
   The welcome few inches of lawn to sit on
         after fourteen miles afoot.
   Smile lines, happy tension in my bones.
   Sopping up energy from workers who believed
         they could change their miserable working conditions.
   Feeling insulted that the governor left town
         rather than welcome us as planned.
   And sensing César was just another worker
         no big cheese
         No pretense of anything more than a spokesman.

LIES

About this time,
rumors fly around the valley
like mosquitoes.
Some say
"Chávez makes piles of money."
Hah!
Five dollars a week plus rent, a few expenses paid
cast-off clothing
some donated food—mostly canned and bagged stuff
of suburban white folks' diets.
Not much for César
Helen
their children
Fernando, Sylvia, Eloise, Linda,
Paul, Anna, Elizabeth, and Anthony.

THE MANY FACES OF A CRUSADER
October, 1967

César and Episcopal Bishop James Pike
on stage
revving up city folk to send dollars
for the strike fund.
Pike smooth, oh so smooth his words strut
"sitting next to my hero, César Chávez,"
next to quiet understatements César makes.

Just before 11:00
says the clock on our Nova wagon's dashboard.
Quiet in the back seat
César nuzzled up against Helen
catnaps.
Late
but the students waited
waited to glean from their mentor
how nonviolence works in Delano
so they can duplicate those tools in the big city.

One-thirty in the morning
we push through the doors of Cantor's.
"This place is great; you'll love it."
César moves into the restaurant as if
he'd just swung through the front door at home.
Must have come here when he worked in L.A.,
reorganizing the political premises and priorities
in *los barrios.*
Semicircular leather booths surprise
more plush than appropriate for our tribe.

César's order comes
he spoons obnoxious-looking brown stuff
  onto my plate—
"Chopped chicken liver. My favorite."
I try
am hooked for life.

Saturday, a rally
supporting for governor
Edmund G. "Pat" Brown
the man who snuck out of meeting farm workers
on the capitol steps that Easter morning
after the long march from Delano to Sacramento.
Political pies—a mix of strange ingredients.

Next, Watts.
César offers a small group
African- and Mexican-Americans
a pep talk
beginning with "Thank you. Thank you for
letting me come be with you, brothers and sisters."
He strolls around the room
with pleasure.
A couple of boys confess
they've been in on the violence in Watts.
César answers their questions
about the use of force
with great understanding
explains without judgement

that destruction simply isn't
the best use of one's energy.
"You can do it. If you want to, you can
do whatever you want. You can get power
without violence. You should try it."
After supper, a TV interview taping
César shines
the bashful boy of the Pike panel gone
confident leader in his place.

At day's end I am sure
that *La Causa*,
The Cause,
is for all people.

HOLY GHOSTS
January 1, 1968

The year begins
with César, Jim, Richard
huddled over a Mankalah board in our living room,
moving the little pebbles from hole to hole.
Jim whoops
"César, I beat you."
Father John is glued to the Rose Bowl game.

Revelries die down.
Before César leaves, he asks Jim
"Can we have a special Mass here tonight?
To start off the New Year. Just a few families."
That evening four families and a couple of single people
fill every chair, overflow onto our floor.
The Franciscan Father Mark Day
schoolboy in frock, freckles and dark-rimmed glasses
uses headlines for liturgy
after which we say
"Lord have mercy."
What surely the bishop wouldn't understand is
the inclusion of a now-married ex-priest
and a Protestant minister
but Jesus would have loved it!

Mid-solemnity
our cat picks her way
along the ivories of the old piano in our carport.
The dissonant tune she plays
is accompanied by two laughs

one a cackle—César's
one with the edges sanded—Richard's.
Forty-something years to my eyes
ten-year-olds at heart.
"Remember, Rookie," César whispers,
"The night the ghost played the piano
when we were little?"
Richard leaks a little smile
squirms at the interruption of Mass.
"Yeah."
Like characters out of a novel
by Isabel Allende or Gabriel Garcia Marquez
these brothers straddle the spirit world.

FEEDING THE SPIRIT
February–March 10, 1968

I.   Picket line tempers percolate.
A striker with no family
nothing particular to live for, he says
vows to kill a grower.

On the off chance
he can change the man's mind
César goes on a water-only fast,
his retreat a room out at The Forty Acres.

II.   Endless prayers.
Grape strikers
and workers striving in other crops
line up nightly
some with home-garden flowers in hand
—a quarter-mile queue on weekends—
to visit César before Mass.
A cot is set up for him in the room he had hoped
would be the gas station's storage closet.
His tenacity clutches hearts.

I get in the waiting line one night
heart pounding
what shall I say to him?
My turn.
Ushered in
door closes.
César lies on a cot
bundled in winter-hooded jacket
zipped to his chin.
More than a dozen tiny hand-made crosses on the wall
one for each day of fasting
gifts from a striker.
Flowers

books
heavy air.
"How are you?"
He says it first.

Each night at Mass he appears
more shrunken
subdued
pale
soon depending on a man at each shoulder
to lift him from his tiny cloister
to the lube bay, turned church for an hour.
He averts his eyes from those who vow
they will not take a life
who promise to work harder
to keep strike and union alive
and César alive,
hagame el favor de comer, oh please *Señor*,
eat.

III.   Twenty-two, twenty-three, twenty-four...
Day twenty-five
limp as a *huelga* flag in fog
César is ferried by friends
to a metal chair in front of a
flatbed truck-altar
at Delano's Garces Park.
Thousands watch this March morning.
Three special people sit alongside
the man who now seems saintly:
The Senator, now simply Bobby,
César's mother Juana, her hummingbird energy stilled,

and César's partner in life
the proud-arched eyebrows
and determined-mouth Helen,
her customary calm off-kilter.
This year, this strike, this union
a life she could not have anticipated
eight children and many houses before today.

The day spins with red flags, guitar strums,
clap clapclap clapclapclapclap
Viva Chávez, Viva la unión
festival sounds to drown anxiety about
the jaundiced, lifeless man
without whom we may not win.

Our leader's bony fingers accept a piece of bread
baked in homes by women faithful to social justice
blessed by the priest for communion
loaves rich with devotion, their main ingredient.

In that multitude
it is almost embarrassing to watch
César's private signal to his Lord.
Breath comes more easily to onlookers,
to us his family
he will be all right now.

IV.   Afternoon's warmth lifts the flavor
of this potpourri
Music
Applause
Relief
Reverence
Earnest speeches
Words of allegiance and faith
Recommitment
to preservation of life.

V.   Monday's *Delano Record* issues an epilogue
quoting the mayor,
"It's a big fraud."
And grape grower Martin Zaninovich,
"The fast was a veiled threat
of violence. But
it is a hollow threat."

THE
C
R
O
S
S

The cross
at The Forty Acres
Telephone poles Richard put together
boasts roses
celebrates
Easter
sun
rise.

Dark hood of night
forty-eight hours later
an enemy of farm worker justice
hacks it down
pours
gasoline
on
it
torches
it.

CRAZY

Maria
tossed ashore from the Chilean revolution
stands in the doorway
of the rented Pink House
its converted bedroom-to-office entrance
her navy wool sweater tired
her shoulders heavy with best intentions
Mutters,
"I no know what to do.
César, he say
I must do this
right away.
LeRoy, he say
César say
you must do this other thing
right away.
What I do?"

She whips around
hoping I don't see her tears
says
"César Chávez is crazy."

I talk to her proud back
"*Sí*, and the sooner you learn that
the easier it will be
to work here."

CAROLINA VASQUEZ
EARLY UNION MEMBER

*Her singing at the end of each day during
the march to Sacramento is unforgettable*
1966

© *John A. Kouns*

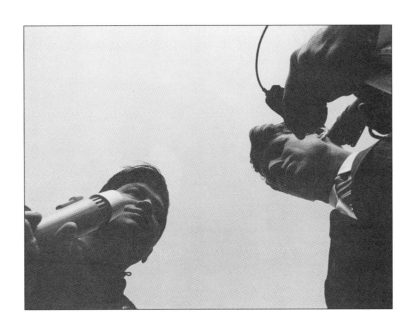

S E N A T O R   R O B E R T   K E N N E D Y

came to Delano to hold a hearing
stayed in the hearts of farm workers
1966

© *Jon Lewis*

B R E A K I N G   T H E   2 6 – D A Y   F A S T

LEFT to RIGHT front row:
wife Helen Chávez, friend Robert Kennedy
César, mother Juana Chávez

back row: V.P. Andy Imutan
two I don't recall
Union Co-founder, Larry Itliong
V.P. Julio Hernandez
Pete Cardenas
V.P. Philip Vera Cruz
(peeking over Larry's and
Julio's shoulders)
1968

© *John A. Kouns*

PORTRAIT

1969

© *Bob Fitch*

ANOTHER HARVEST
Coachella, California—May, 1968

Another grape harvest,
another strike.
Desert lands inherited from the moon,
ranges draped in several shades
blue
purple
mauve
Yet across the valley
as the sun ripens,
camel-colored.
An occasional palm tree stands impertinent.
Wearisome sage brush and tumbleweed
become a luxury of turquoise-grey laciness.
The ocotillo,
sparsely clad,
a lookout for tiny birds
scanning skies for breakfast.
Still, rock lovers could lose their fascination—
too much of too little.

Then the eye catches the deep green vineyards.
Grape growers have wrought a miracle
with waters stolen from the north
to convert desert into verdant fertility.

ADIÓS, AMBASSADOR OF HOPE
Los Angeles, California—June 5, 1968

Who really knows why
Senator Robert Kennedy
forged a powerful link
with César.
Politics, yes.
Easier to believe though
they envisioned similar pictures
of America's future.

Just as the Ambassador Hotel ball room
exploded with victory
after the Presidential candidate's grateful speech,
shots rang out, muffled
by the din of celebrants.
For an hour, whispers of
"Have you seen César?"
floated among the stunned.

After eons
   in the hotel parking lot
   in a motel room watching doctors' reports
after tossing and turning on a lumpy mattress
after passing up breakfast
Jim and I found our way to campaign headquarters.
César said he had watched on TV last night,
keeping Helen company.
It was said she had molded boycotters
into a get-out-the-vote team,
led the victory.
Hard at first for me to imagine her,
my so-private coworker in the credit union,

rallying hoards of campaigners,
though no one ever doubted her determination.

That afternoon
César, Helen, Jim, Dolores and I stop
on our way back to Delano
for lunch in Bakersfield at Bill Lee's restaurant.
(Dolores missed flying bullets by inches.)
César picks at his favorite Chinese food
searches for what to tell strikers
now that their friend in high places is gone.
Searches for hope
without a brother in the struggle.

INSECURITY
1968

A weasel of a man confesses
someone's out to get César.
Big valley grower money
spread on the table
to stop this renegade
who says he's organizing a union
but it don't look like that to
the rednecks in the valley.

Locked doors
drawn shades
seized-up nerves
twenty-four-hour patrols,
though
Malcolm Jack Bobby Martin proved to us
bodyguards don't stop bullets.

PORTRAIT—1969

Forty-two years line his face,
especially the crinkles at eyes' edge,
handsome.
Under his eyes,
pressures,
pain,
age sneaks up,
but the chin remains resolute,
lips full and gentle.
Sometimes
the crow-black hair
flops in unkempt strands
a lower priority these jam-packed days.
The cardigan sweater is now a uniform,
its gentian-violet color reminding me
of the stuff Mom used to put on my skinned knees.
Helen and their girls keep César in
well-ironed plaid cotton shirts and khaki or brown work pants.

At The Forty Acres, late one afternoon,
I introduce César to my father.
They face each other
mirrors
eye contact at eye level.
Phallic-lensed cameras around their necks.
A German Shepherd on a leash at each man's side
behaving with full grasp of their masters' expectations.
The men speak easily.
It's hard to say
who is more charming.
It isn't the first time I see
how much César reminds me of Dad.

UNSYMPATHETIC ABOUT SYMPATHY
Spring, 1969

César says that
in spite of growing support for the boycott,
freshened with the onset of a new harvest,
"Nothing happens
if all we have are
warehouses of sympathy."

Now Everyone Knows Who He Is

Time magazine.
July 4, 1969
César on the cover.
Wow.

"For most of them [the people around Chávez], Chávez is a
symbol rather than a person... César reluctant to talk of self,
only *la causa*... Mystical mien with peasant earthiness."

part three

CLOSE UP

A person of courage is also full of faith.

—Cicero

I Have Been Sitting Too Long
January 26–February 7, 1970

Farther away from home than I have ever been,
in New Delhi, half-way round the world from my babies,
Jim and I, César's emissaries. Our leader's bad back and full calendar
wouldn't tolerate this trip for a seminar
celebrating Mahatma Gandhi's hundredth birthday.

One lunchtime, between pontificating meetings, I am shopping.
Handcrafted necklaces, only a dollar, splayed over burlap on the
sidewalk. A little brown-eyed wonder approaches, touches my
elbow, pushes her shoe box into my peripheral vision, removes the
lid. In this box, scrawny chicken left to bake too long?

No.

Brown, motionless newborn.

I put a dollar in sister's hand, turn away,
walk tear-blurred trail back to the Gandhi Peace Center.

That night I listen to Vietnamese Buddhist Thich Nhat Hanh,
to T.Y. Rogers, who worked with Martin Luther King, to my
husband, César Chávez' right-hand man. They consider how to
inspire people to promote social change without coming to blows.
Thich Nhat Hanh, in leaden near-whisper, says his people
cannot think, cannot talk, with so much killing around them.

I am the only woman.

I sit. I have been sitting too much the past three days.

Afraid I will scream if I hear one more *should* or *could*,
in the midst of philosophizing I announce that we peace-makers
must proclaim our opposition to the slaughter in Vietnam,
declare it is time for giant powers to back off, so the Vietnamese can
settle their uncivil civil chaos. I have an idea for how we might be
heard in Moscow, in China, heard in Vietnam, in Washington, D. C.
We can get people at this seminar to march, go to the embassies,
plead for withdrawal from Vietnam.

The men pat me on the head with words.

My cautious husband that night says *Don't*.

That big "No" hurls me into action. César has spoken in this
seminar through Jim; now it's my turn to follow the Chávez lead.

Next morning I find a phone—not so easy in India—call our
embassy, newspapers, map out with T.Y. and Thich Nhat Hanh
a march to the U.S. Embassy, sadly realizing we have no entree,
no language to speak with China and U.S.S.R. ambassadors.

Though *Don't* keeps arising, on the appointed day, fifty conferees
line up behind Buddhist priests and nuns,
follow us past the rich red door of the Chinese embassy,
on to the gull-grey concrete of our own.

We have an appointment, yet an uninformed guard slams a lock
on the wrought-iron opening.

The ambassador's stand-in arrives, stares down the snaking line,
orders the gates opened, saying,
"There are too many of you. We have room only for a few."

As we pass through the gates, he asks the Buddhists to stop their
noise, stop tapping their prayer wheels with sticks.
Jim turns his rarely disdainful eye on the stand-in.
"They are praying, praying for you."

Our meeting is civil.
Mr. Stand-in promises to convey our message to President Nixon.

Next morning, front page New Delhi newspapers,
"Gates shut on peace group," "Cease-fire in Vietnam."
Large photographs of the march.

I glide with new wings. Lining up to be counted
is what Gandhi wanted for the people of India,
what César wants for farm workers.

Courage, bravery, chutzpah—watery words for this
all-too-magic adrenaline time when the gods applaud
those who work in spite of.

74

DAYS OF EMPATHY
Spring 1970

How alone some days must feel
suffering with back pain
unresolved strikes.
The squeeze is on.
Lines etch César's face
eyes sad
the leader exhausted
shuttling from Delano
running the union
then off to contract negotiations
to turn enemies into co-operators
The long skinniness of California
spreads meetings far apart
spreads energy thin.

As if that isn't enough,
The National Labor Relations Board announces that,
unless a voluntary settlement is obtained,
the Board will issue unfair labor practice complaints
for promoting the grape boycott.

They say he is David
against Goliath landowners.
Yet today's Goliath has brothers in
the Imperial Valley
in Delano
Sacramento
Washington, DC.
Job would surely slap an arm
over César's shoulders,
say, "I know how you feel."

LA VICTORIA
July 29, 1970

"I am convinced
that this country can be changed
non-violently.
I see it in my people's eyes."

César quotes Gandhi: "Suffering
   in one's own person,
   instead of rendering violence to others,
   is the essence of non-violence.
   I cannot teach it to cowards.
   It is the summit of bravery."

Wet-behind-the ears negotiators
and contract administrators
somehow
get hundreds of farm workers
and peace
back to the vineyards.

Five years of waiting
waiting for the day
to celebrate.
Jim and I, stuck on the boycott
in Columbus, Ohio sticky-summer,
not invited to the fiesta in Delano.
No money to make the drive anyway.

Joy—diluted—
all but dissolves
days later.
Another strike
this time the lettuce fields of Salinas.
From treasured assistant to
"Wait to see where we need you next,"
Jim broods, homely with what-next questions
on the outside looking in.
I meet helplessness head-on.

EL JEFE IN THE BIG APPLE
November 30, 1970

Our Chief visits the New York staff.
Reassigned from the heart of *La Huelga*
to the cornerstone boycott city
Jim and I shiver there.

I want to go back to Delano.
I'm not happy to see our boss.
Our family is holed up in the attic apartment
of a boycott supporter's house;
by day I am her maid
by night I am lonesome.

Saturday night, my first close-up
a groupie kind of thing
following César.
Hotel Commodore
a Puerto Rican Civil Rights dinner
an award on behalf of the union.

Sunday morning, Riverside Church.
Thousands pack into pews,
"Ohs" and "ahs" swell up from the sympathetic
when César
without drama
lays out details:
accidents
pesticide misuse
leaking roofs
inadequate nutrition.
Nearby
in the parishioners' own back yard
New Jersey farm workers face even worse
wages, housing, working conditions.

After church
boycotters young and old
hang on the labor leader's every word.
César says he's going to jail in Salinas
to protest an injunction against the picketing.
Lettuce-growing giants
hand-in-hand with Teamsters
are at our union's throat again,
cozying up to growers,
promising to keep workers out of their hair.

Sunday evening, a benefit
for the Hospital Workers' Union
honoring Paul Robeson.
Jim and I walk in with César and the audience,
sighting that little Mexican man
I once wrote home about,
breaks into applause.
César sits next to me
talks of my children and
how Helen misses me working in the credit union.
I can't stay cynical or frosty
in his presence.

Robeson Junior says, he supposes
we stand the chance of César getting treatment
similar to his Dad's
if our country heads further right in the next few years.
"It was Congressman Richard Nixon who led the witch-hunt
that ended with my father losing his passport."

It's easy to shelve that risk as Dizzy Gillespie,
Ossie Davis and Peter, Paul and Mary takes turns on stage.
During intermission—Mary and César—emerge from
their respective restrooms at the same time and
Mary, it's all she can do not to hug the man.

ON THE ROAD AGAIN
January 19, 1971

Out of the Salinas jail, César's back in Manhattan to file a lawsuit
—this time against the Defense Department for buying lettuce,
for helping break the latest strike.

At a demonstration, Bella Abzug's crazy hat bobs among
hard hats in the crowd of the rallying supporters.

Later Jim and I follow César from print shop to print shop
in search of the perfect press for putting out the union's flyers
and posters. César slings the jargon of ink and press around
as if he's been in the business for decades.

Up at a supporter's Central Park West apartment, his white-
socked feet move across the thick carpet as easily as his more
determined strides walk dusty roads of labor camps. Before a
David Frost interview, a quick supper of soy beans with Muenster
cheese and onions. César's traded chopped chicken liver and
Diet-Rite colas for vegetarian delicacies and carrot juice.

In the elevator at the TV station, doors open on a Black man who
bursts into shocked joy, extends his hand with "Mr. Chávez,
Mr. Chávez?" The pump of the man's hand in César's underlines
the smile on his face. "Wait 'til I tell my wife I met César
Chávez!" César asks his name, a bit about his life as sincerely
eager as if beginning a long friendship. They will probably never
meet again, yet their connection will survive.

UNFITTING
March 10, 1971

During one of America's snowiest weeks
Jim drove our little family back to Delano.
In the frozen chaos, I felt kinship with bellied-up semis.
So alone in that too-quiet car.

Jim took off for Salinas soon as he dropped
the boys and me off in Delano
at a house not our own.
I squeezed into offices where needed
not fitting just right.

NUESTRA SEÑORA DE LA PAZ
(OUR LADY OF PEACE)
1971, Keene, California
Headquarters of the United Farm Workers, AFL-CIO,
and Farm Workers Service Center

I.   Few people driving east on Highway 85 from Bakersfield
notice Keene's little store, half-dozen houses
hunkered in close to the four-lane byway.
Keene, California,
usually known for two things:
the railroad switchback
ten miles west of Tehachapi
because it's the most unusual in the state
and La Paz
because it is headquarters for the biggest farm labor union
in the country.

Mountains outline La Paz,
shelter us
from reality outside the work of building
a viable, powerfully effective *union de campesinos.*
More than The Forty Acres,
La Paz becomes The Man's dream
of bringing the universe to a graspable microcosm.

Rocks along the creek
become seats for meditators,
the stream itself gurgling with
courses for the kids' scrap-wood boats,
refreshment for the soul in springtime.
In summer, the creek bed thirsts for winter rains,
reminding us that
for every thing there is a season.

Chilly evenings define Fall.
Some winters, snow powders surrounding hillsides
like giant crullers.

Diesel scents argue all year long with
wafts of fresh grass
or drying rose petals
as freight trains lumber through day and night.

We are hooked on dramatic events, crises and victories, so
we need Mother Nature to tend us
like a beneficent nanny
nudge us to execute the mundane,
to brush the teeth, do the laundry of the union
typing contracts
accounting for contributions
paying bills
answering piles of letters
the stuff of fourteen-hour workdays.

II.   Nature struck magnificence in the hillsides, the creek.
But man used a cheaper architect.
Winter cuts through white wooden walls
green-shingled roofs barely endure the rains.
All is now quaint, bordering on dilapidated.
Reminds me of outdated military installations
instead of the TB sanitarium these buildings housed
before the union arrived.
Staff residences dot earthquake-torn roads.
A place on its way to looking like
a neglected labor camp.

The only building with human activity
is long, rectangular
with a plain porch and stairway up the front.
Inside, wooden floors hint at old-fashioned good taste.

César has set up office
in a smallish corner room,
its windows looking into the lap of endless mountains.
Sun polishes each small pane of glass.

Behind a bright red homemade desk,
El Jefe's rocking lawnchair
prescribed by Dr. Janet Travell the way
she did for Jack Kennedy's bad back.
Small piles of paper look tended to.
Is he here to stay?

III.   He is.
Jim took César's secretary to Coachella,
something to do with the opening grape harvest.
Jim promised, "Just two weeks," then he'd return the woman.
In the meantime Marie Flores would help me
know what to do.
Marie resigned soon to tend her small children and
my two weeks stretched.

César is moving all central administration
to the mountains.
I must move or give up
the job that all my other jobs
have prepared me for
beginning when I was eight
helping Daddy in his law office.
My sons will bus into Tehachapi
learn in a nest of rednecks.
I don't want to move but
Matthew and Tommy see
rocks to climb, rattlesnakes to torment,
rivers in the creek bed,
a salvageable swimming pool,
abandoned buildings complete with bats—
unfenced male freedom
easily imagined by eight- and ten-year-olds.

HAPPY BIRTHDAY
March 31, 1971

"Surprise!"
Helen has organized staff to drive up to La Paz
for César's forty-fourth birthday.
Spring's prancing
radiant orange poppies
regal lupine
tumble down the mountains
either side of the highway climbing
out of the great San Joaquin Valley.

He likes the old TB sanitarium;
Helen doesn't.
Having lived here as a child
she vows never to move up into these hills again.
She brought a huge cardboard card;
on the front is a picture of their grandchild,
inside are all the Delano staff's signatures.
We find our undaunted trailblazer
meeting in the conference room of the Admin building.
Within minutes, he pulls candles
from one of the three gigantic cakes
licks the frosting from each candle.
Someone comments
no pictures have been taken with the candles on the cake
so he pokes them back in.
I like the Little Kid in him; this feels like home.

GREYHOUNDS OR ALBATROSSES

Jim and I moved from Delano to La Paz.
I am working on being a good wife.
I like it here,
love being in the hub of things—
César's secretary.
But my husband's off in L.A.
picking up yet a third huge arthritic Greyhound bus
so César can bring workers
from around California to La Paz,
drive them to political hot-spots for demonstrations,
off to the latest boycott.
Those wheezing monsters
in months to come
choke the Service Center's budget.
Like beached whales their ailments stink
and so does my husband's perpetual absence.

part four

Even Harder Times

Each time a man or woman stands up for justice, the heavens sing and the world rejoices. Each time a man or woman stands up for justice and is struck down, the heavens weep.... We do not need to destroy to win. We are a movement that builds and does not destroy.

César at Nagi Daifullah's funeral
August 17, 1973

DEATH KNOCKS
January 25, 1972

The day is young. I hear you, César,
lay the phone receiver back in its cradle on your desk,
then your footsteps,
and from the office doorway your words come
evenly,
firmly,
quietly:
"Call everyone to the conference room—right away."
Tears blur your eyes.

Minutes later, the staff gathers—
no chairs, the room dim with morning light.
"One of our sisters
has been killed
in Florida, on the picket line.
Her name is Nan Freeman, a Jewish girl. She's...
was
just 19.
Run over by a semi leaving the orange groves.
An accident—probably. Who knows?"
Whispered reactions fill the room.
"Let us pray."
You stretch your arms
out to the people on either side of you
bow your head.
The rest of us move in
complete the circle.

You call the Freemans later that week
after their private memorial service at home.
On the phone with them
you mostly listen
then say
how much you appreciate
Nan's sacrifice
their family's sacrifice.
Your voice trembles.

Some weeks later,
during an afternoon stretch,
you wander over to my desk.
"What are you doing?" you ask
the same way a three-year-old did once
when she saw me with a broom in my hand.
I pass up the chance to be smart-aleck.

You look over my shoulder
at the contract page I'm typing,
then start in on the subject of Jews again,
a continuation of our conversation the year before
when I'd reminded you half my genes are Jewish.
"All the growers have Jewish attorneys.
I think I'll change my name so
they'll be more impressed in negotiations.
From now on, I'll be Chávezstein."
Such a naughty chuckle follows
as you try to fill in that aching space
carved by the loss of Nan.

Too Much
1972

The juggling act requires a half-dozen
Césars.
Automating the accounting,
setting up the print shop,
developing a mailing list
for instant gratification
whenever funds need to be rallied.
Gotta have staff cars
hooked on Dodge Darts
to buy
and then repair
and repair
and repair
and then...

More and more people
around the country notice him
want to know who this guy is
wielding nonviolence
instead of fists;
what chance does he have
up against California's biggest income-producers?
Media moguls come panting
drive him up and down the state,
just to grab news.
The German Shepherds—Red, Boycott and Huelga—
turn mournful manipulative eyes,
plead for scratches behind their ears,
for kindness their friend used to have time to give.

FASTING AGAIN: ARIZONA
May, 1972

"As far as I'm concerned, these people do not exist,"
says Arizona Governor Jack Williams
who made a law to give unions a rough time organizing.
He says that to farm workers
right to their faces.

César retaliates
with a "fast of love," a "fast of sacrifice"
hoping to soften the governor's heart
embolden the workers' earnestness
somehow assuage the fear of those
who have no sympathy for laborers.

Jim moves to Arizona
masterminds the campaign to Recall the Governor.
I take our sons to visit.

Soon as the boys pile into their Daddy's arms
I wind my way through dozens of workers
milling about in the Santa Rita Community Center
readying to go door to door to register voters,
enter a small room where César lies on a high bed
his face yellow in the eerie light.

Thinking he is sleeping
I kiss his forehead.
He opens his eyes
murmurs "Glad you're here,"
a small curve to his lips.
His hair
mussed and dry
lies in undignified mats across his scalp
and down the back of his neck.

A white sheet weighs heavily.
What little water his body consumes
oozes through his pores—
it's too hot in here.

"I just wanted to see you," I whisper back
and turn to leave.
He fumbles for my hand.
"Don't go yet.
Tell me,
how are the boys? Did they come with you?"

He rolls from side to stomach
buries his face against his arm
pain somewhere
He searches for cordiality and bravery.
I answer his questions.
He drags his sandpaper tongue over his lips,
chapping too far gone for relief.
He wants to see Matthew and Tommy.

"Sister, could you hand me the water?"
Each sip agonizing.
I don't see him swallow.
"And the office?
How are things at La Paz?"

My voice swells with renewed buoyancy.
at the distraction.
"It's fine.
I guess everyone knows you're here—they don't call."
He says, "No, not many here either. Maybe
they can do without me."

I squeeze his hand.
If he has notions of being dispensable
I can't second them.
"Sí se puede."
"What?"
His voice a tiny breeze
against the din crescendoing in the meeting hall.
"*Sí se puede.* That's our new battle cry.
People here, they're not like in California,
the people here don't believe the union
can make a difference. They say
No se puede it can't be done."

Maybe they were right:
the Gov sat out his term,
the law wasn't changed.
But the people were.
The people were.

BROTHERLY BOOST
June 29, 1972

Jim and I separated—
put words to what had been
for years.
Him, focused;
Me, kaleidoscopic.
He told César and Helen
the day César broke his fast.

Back in La Paz,
César is welcomed with
stacks of mail
a mound of pink phone message slips.
Instead of tackling them
he interrupts, "Come with me."

I follow my boss to sit on boulders
in the sunshine by the rose garden
in front of the Administration Building.
He looks down at his hands
says he and Helen are devastated
by the break-up of Jim's and my marriage.
Wants to know what he can do.
Says "Men find you attractive
you are vulnerable now; be careful."

What could be attractive
about my perpetually tear-swollen eyes?
What would men like
about the whining and bitching
that hit me with locomotive force
from time to time these days?

César says he's sorry
he missed the surprise birthday party Helen gave me
asks my age.
When I say "thirty-four"
he does that fingers-to-lips thing
that chefs do about a luscious recipe
and says, "That's when a woman peaks—
ripe and beautiful."

FATHER OF THE GROOM
September 15, 1972

Helen and the Chávez kids
have gone to Delano
to finish last minute preparations.
Tomorrow
the first-born Chávez, Fernando,
will marry.

César asks for my company.
When my first-born marries
many years later
I understand what I did not that evening—
that perhaps he felt as if a piece of him
was floating away.

No fire in the man this night, though
the air is an oven in the hours
just before the sun stops lighting the sky.
The house smells of
dogs
the guard's cigarette
cilantro.
A radio plays.

César talks of wanting more children
a fresh start at fatherhood.
His wistfulness is raw.

RACKING UP
October 22-24, 26-28, 1972

Foes pen Proposition 22
nastily outlawing boycotts
strikes
the tools of this trade.
César hits San Francisco and Los Angeles
bulging calendar stuffed in his pocket.
Says he's worn out Mary Jean as a go-fer
sends for me.
By nightfall I am exhausted,
he's invigorated.
Union meetings
TV tapings
phone calls
frantic freeways
student rallies
delayed meatless suppers and then

a pool hall where brother against brother
Richard and César go at it
the way I imagine they did as kids
back in Arizona
when the table clicked with billiard balls by daylight
and became the two little boys' bed at night.
The joking.
César taunting and teasing
so his adversary's cue slides off the ball.
Hooting over a winning shot
César shuts out growers
workers
onlookers.

A giddy-buffoon sparkle in his eyes,
a big brotherly strut
when he beats Rookie.

Crafty at the pool table
it seems as if to César
people are like these colorful spheres
only instead of a cue
he shoots with common sense
encouragement
appreciation.

EDUCATION

César greets workers,
their labor scrubbed clean,
white shirts and fresh trousers.
Members bused to La Paz for the weekend.
He welcomes them as if this is their new "home."
Once the workers settle down in the conference room
he tells them
about his Arizona childhood days,
his parents' courageous leap into the migrant stream,
how he met Fred Ross and went to work for the CSO.
Then he talks about leaving CSO,
starting the National Farm Workers' Association.
From our office, I hear his voice intensify
when he speaks
of having no weapons on the picket lines
in spite of the workers' fears
for their safety—and his.

One time in a La Paz community meeting,
César talked about education,
educacion,
as street smarts,
common sense,
learning by the seat of your pants.
Yet he reads and reads
beats the sun up
so he can read some more,
because he believes self-*educacion* is as necessary
as anything bought in college.

WIN SOME, LOSE SOME
November, 1972

> *We won Prop 22 by a "narrow" margin*
> *of some one million votes! But*
> *Nixon is President again...*

Some growers renew contracts, but
the six-year-old contract with Schenley ends.

DANCING IN THE EYE OF THE STORM
December 31, 1972

Great New Year's Eve dance
filling the La Paz kitchen (a.k.a. our dance hall),
staff grumbling set aside
by infectious conviviality.

César, you may struggle with *mujeres*—
we insist on being heard—
but you love our attention
keep on spinning around the floor
with as many different women as possible.
That's one of the great things about La Paz dances.
Three-year-olds and sixty-three-year-olds
take turns with you
gyrating to jitterbug, rock,
floating to slow-dance melodies.

You're the D.J. that night
Anyone else wants to choose the next tune,
you first pass judgment on the choice.
After a couple of glasses of wine,
you aren't apt to say "no."
How you love lavishing your hosting skills on us,
tu familia.

CÉSAR AND
JUANA ESTRADA CHÁVEZ

*at a march in Modesto, California
part of the campaign to get Gallo wines
back under contract
1975*

SEÑOR ZAPATA

*at a Friday night union meeting
expressing gratitude to the union
for repairing his car so he could
continue going to picket
late 1960s*

© *John A. Kouns*

TOM, SUSAN, MATTHEW
AND JIM DRAKE

circa 1969

Photographer unknown

A SENSE OF JUSTICE

© John A. Kouns

Papa Bear and How He Got His Name

They say
that family is made up of those people
who are
always
there for you
when you need them.

If that's true, then
you,
father brother son friend but
especially father César,
deserve to be called Papa Bear.
You and I share that love of nicknames.
Image-wise, ahem, you've become a little round—more
teddy-bearish.

But it's really much more than appearance.
I survey this collage of humanity
your staff
think how you shepherd us.
Some wouldn't like to admit that but
look, this is a family of sorts:
The man born so late in his Dad's life
he received little fatherly mentoring
and seeks it from you.
The daughter of alcoholics whose
culinary offerings sustained you during the Salinas strike.

The woman raped on the St. Louis boycott.
The picker with lost fingers.
The refugee from Chilé's horrors.
The too-soon pregnant.
The gambling addict.
The rigid and the loose.
All looking for
something they miss from home
or perhaps never knew.

So Human

One warm afternoon
you take a break
rubbing your neck
stretching
next to my desk.
I blurt out
"You are the most Christ-like person
I've ever met."

You choke me.
From behind a devilish grin spills,
"Just so you know I'm not."

PERSUASION

Farm workers
All races
Ages
Flannel-suitors
Hollywood stars
Singers internationally known
César tucks them so neatly
into the pocket
of the movement.

In crowded auditoriums
he talks as if each listener is
the only one who matters
as if he's sitting on his little red desk-top,
one leg on the floor for support,
tugging with one hand on the fingers of the other
just telling us how it is.

Or pacing across the room
so we have to tennis-match watch
hanging on each word
each liveliness in his eyes
each sad screen
the determined jaw.
He doesn't talk at us.

We hunker down together
planning,
imagining,
cursing,
promising
girding with quiet resolve his casual inclusivity.

Who wouldn't do just about anything for this man?
Not because, as he hopes, he speaks for God
but more likely because he is
a piece of God.

DOGFIGHT

Red and Huelga lack their owner's commitment
to nonviolence.
La Paz
often erupts
in a barrage of barking and growling
just before César's two closest friends leap
onto one another, ripping ferociously.

César shouts.
Commands.
They won't stop.
The infuriated Shepherds tear at each other

Yelping,
The Boys, as Helen named them,
stop only
when someone grabs them from behind
squeezing their most vulnerable place.
The proud warriors whimper
lick their wounds.
Saliva and crimson mat their coats
until evening when César goes home for dinner
combs their luxurious fur,
gentles his pals with soft words.

MORNING OASIS

High above La Paz' purring creek
in macho splendor
rise mammoth tors
their jaggedness
stitched with rusty lichen.

Each morning that he's at La Paz
César escapes his bodyguards—
except the dogs—
climbs the dawn
into nearly vertical hills,
temple of stone.

Each step lifts him
away from demands
lets his heart soar
like the gliding hawks overhead.

Here he sorts matters of the heart
messages from his Maker
drinks courage
generates strength.

IRE SIGNS
March 5, 1972

I return from a weekend in Palo Alto
find my office phone
dead on the floor.
Someone pulled it out of the wall.

I ask to have it fixed
and Al tells me
that you yanked it out, César,
because you were irate
that I was gone two weekends
in a row.
How childish!
Damn you!

You finally talk to me about it.
That familiar position with your hands
parallel
a few inches apart
fingers splayed
their parentheses focusing your thoughts.
It's hard not to look at your hands
harder to look into your eyes
for anger
or forgiveness.
"You made me look bad with Chris Hartmire."
"*I* wasn't the one who ripped the phone out of the wall,"
my heart beats fast with furious disbelief;
"I *had* to talk to somebody about it."

Then my favorite
infuriating
unpredictable
boss lowers his eyes from mine.

"I tore the phone out
because you took off again.
Why?"

Blustering with indignation, I explain.
"...my Grandpa,
a sermon at the Presbyterian Church in Palo Alto
about the union."

Your eyes cloud mean. "You're not
qualified to speak on behalf of the union—
not to important supporters like those."

I refuse to argue that
when I was on the boycott
qualifications didn't matter.

"But that was my congregation as a child...
long-time friends saw to it that I spoke."
I remind you, "You said it was fine to visit my grandfather..."

You stage whisper
"How could I tell you no?"
then regain your boss-role. "It just
makes me mad
when I'm expected to do without you for a day.

Mary Jean wasn't here either."
Ah,
so that's it.
You had to fend for yourself!

CAN YOU IMAGINE

Papa Bear, you always say
"Can you imagine…"
"Can you imagine…"
Big, big dreams you unwind for us
with those words.

I adore you
like so many other workers on your staff
like so many workers in the fields
I adore you.
But can you ever imagine
how much you hurt me
those days
you snap my spirit
into pieces too jagged to pick up easily?

Still, I suppose I must imagine how you feel
when your helpers say, "*No se puede*"
when we say, "You're doing it wrong."
We used to expect you
to prune and thin,
keep us watered.

The time has come
when we imagine
when we think for ourselves.

LOYAL MEANS WHAT?
April 3, 1973

Another day, another run-in.
Pacing the hardwood floor in your office,
your back to me,
you say, "You should have
stood up for me. Supported me."

I wait
until you face me.
"I will support you if I agree with you,
but not if I don't."

The muscles in your jaw tighten.
"Why aren't you loyal to me?"

I'm shocked.
"I *am* loyal to you
but not always to what you say."

Then I understand
that for you
because we are family
For you
that bond supersedes all others.

But in my family
what feels *right* supersedes, even
when it means going against a relative.

RAM & CRAB

"Susan, what sign are you?"
I hate it when you call me Susan
instead of Susanita; it means
you're annoyed with me.
"What do you mean, what sign?"
"When's your birthday?"
"June twenty-fifth."

Your brow rolls into a furious, knowing *aha*
"Dammit. That explains it. Your
water's trying to put out my fire."
You pivot away from me
rifle among stacks of paper on your desk.
"It's astrology Susan. Get a book
read about it. Kerry did my chart. I can't find my
chart. I'm Aries with Leo."

I could care less
until I pick up Linda Goodman's *Sun Signs* in the book store.
You're right.
Like fingernails on a blackboard, some of our days are
but now I see why.
It's a battle for me to color inside the lines
of traditional office blueprints,
to battle waxing and waning moods in sync with the moon.
You, you're a born leader who struggles
with control and fire,
who tongue-lashes
anyone caving into mood swings
anyone suspected
of not working as hard as you do.
This year it's too bad we don't realize
it takes Aries' fire *and* Cancer's water to cook.

BREAKING THE TYPE CAST

Click click click.
Clickclickclick ring clickclickclick.
Through the door, I see you,
  magnifying half-glasses slid to the end of your nose,
                               typing.
All these years
I thought
that was one thing I could do
that you couldn't.

NONVIOLENCE TESTED
Lamont Grape Harvest, 1973

They call the bruisers
"The Garbage Truck"—
a bunch of goons,
Teamsters or
some guys they hired to scare us.

The sun hasn't quite erased our shivers
one morning when their truck pulls up to our picket line.
Sumo-wrestler types sit on the back of the flat-bed
and maybe seventy-five of us,
office staffers alongside grape tenders,
stop waving skimpy *huelga* flags
stop talking.
The thudding of our hearts
beats out a rhythm of fear.

One goon, belly oozing over his belt,
tidies his greasy black hair,
shoves his comb back in his hind pocket,
picks up a baseball bat and
starts his swaggering journey toward us.
The others don't bother with grooming, just
get on with their strut across the asphalt.

The bat swings
swings again
screams fill the air.
On the road next to the pickup truck,
where I hold little Matthew and Tommy tightly,
a young worker picks up his pruning shears
opens them
and starts down the line toward the bullies.

A tiny, grandmotherly woman
steps in front of him
wraps her arms around him
yells,
"*No, M'ijo! No violencia. César dice
'No violencia.'
Por favor...*"
The warrior drops his shears
smears tears from his cheeks
lets go of the pride his
nineteen-year-old heart carries.

Next thing I hear is
Señor Juan Hernandez' skull hitting the pavement
like a watermelon.
More screams.
The goon chortles,
struts away
from writhing Señor Hernandez.

When the shock wears off I see
The Garbage Truck
has left behind
bodies
blood
shrieks
nausea.

Heavy price to pay
for turning the other cheek:
no stain of violence on our hands.

METTLE

It's the end of a long evening staff meeting.
César finishes by shaking his finger
at the unmarried volunteers,
says quit complaining about housing
—they live in the converted old hospital rooms—
tells them to behave themselves.
Grins,
his gold tooth catching the overhead light.

"You've all seen the picture
Rookie, I mean Richard, put up out front.
The rear-end of a bull with the big..."
He cups his hands, each as if full of
something massive
"...*cojones*.
Sorry, Sisters."
He means all the women in the union family,
not just the nuns.
"That picture is out on the bulletin board
to remind you that
this work takes..."

He stops again,
giggles boyishly
repeats, "Well, go look at the picture."

KNUCKLES

Snap.
Crunch. Crunch.
God, he's
driving
me
CRAZY.

But do you tell a man
whose picture's been on the cover of *Time* magazine
that cracking his knuckles is irritating the hell of you?

I do.
Time or no *Time,*
El Jefe, El Monito,
Charismatic Labor Leader,
whatever.

PAYING A PRICE
August 1973

It's dark in Coachella.
Someone approaches the home of a union member
sets the house afire
burns it to the ground
leaving only a few pots and pans
bedsprings
appliances
writhing in the ashes.

In Brawley,
a picket line captain is beaten to death.
No one knows how it happened.

Someone ignites a fire bomb
in a grape striker's car.

In Bakersfield, after a party
picketers hang out on a street corner.
Cops order them to disperse,
there's a scuffle.
The cop says Nagi ran.
The cop says he had to hit 24-year-old Nagi Daifullah.
Denies the flashlight he subdued Nagi with
was a problem.
Says the hundred-pound Arab kid
just fell to the pavement and
that's what killed him.

Less than a day later,
a scab reacts to union picketing
comes out of a vineyard
gun blazing
cuts down Juan de la Cruz.

TYRANNY OR LOYALTY?
1973

With some intuition and innocence
I approach a couple of UFW lawyers,
the negotiator, some AFL-CIO staff
with my criticisms of César's strategy.
César says we get a contract with the kingpin grower
or nobody gets a contract.

I think
we should keep the few contracts we have
keep members who've risked and
been faithful.
Don't go all or nothing.
Of course it's more complicated—
the big guy owns the cold storage shed.
Where will the little guys store grapes after the harvest?
But that could be worked out.
César's advisors tell me, "You're right but
César won't listen."

I think
because we are friends
because the situation is desperate
that I must try to get César to listen.

He's never in the office anymore—
meetings, important meetings all over the country.
So I write him a letter full of kindness and reason,
make the mistake of naming my supporters
men he trusts.
César believes I have organized a mutiny.

DISMISSED
August 2, 1973

The phone rings.
José listens.
Protests.
Hangs up.
Folds his arms
over the chest of his blue denim work shirt
looks over our back-to-back desks at me.
One hand strays
pushes his heavy-rimmed glasses back up
the bridge of his nose.
"César says you're fired."
Then José says, "You remind me of the kid
in the story The Emperor's New Clothes."

part   five

ON THE OUTSIDE
LOOKING IN

Loss is change and change is Nature's delight. This has been true from the beginning and will be true to the end. Then how can you say it is wrong, forever wrong, that no power in heaven can fix it, and that the world lies condemned to a thralldom of ills unrelenting?

—Marcus Aurelius Antoninus
Emperor of Rome, 161–180 A.D.

A Quiet Port in a Decade of Storms

Ten years of holding fund-raisers,
hearing César's speeches when he's in town,
I use up my fury and frustration.
Understand that he is as human as the rest of us.
Believe the movement might die without him,
know the movement must live beyond pettiness.

Finally with convolutions amuck
César excuses my insurrection
says I was a pawn of male staff.
Insulted
I protest that I conceived the letter idea—
the guys had supported only my reasoning,
they'd warned me not to say anything…
It's just as well he didn't believe me this time.

With our new amnesty, he finds my Palo Alto home
convenient place to retreat
when he's working in the Bay Area.
They show up at all hours—
Mike, more driver and companion than guard these days,
and my stocky, greying friend.
I miss the heavy plaid jacket from the first fast
the purple-navy sweater of the early years.
César's Members-Only jacket offends my nostalgia.

Sometimes I wonder
since my birthday is the day after his mother's
if my nesting ways somehow duplicate hers
and that's why he likes to visit.

These are the years
the media blows icy on the man.
Some staff abandon ship
and perform surgery on the union in public.
He dumps others overboard.
It's been a decade since the first contracts
and now, only a few exist.
Salinas union members, incensed
robbed of their power in *la unión*,
the way they see it,
take César to court.

So we talk of his dreams—
this angel drifting down
down
down—
to wrap him warmly in his future.
One is a newsletter
for all the former staff
"to keep in touch."
Or a magazine. "You be the editor," he says
but takes the job from me before it's barely begun
and lists himself Editor of *Food & Justice*.

Sometimes he daydreams beyond the practical.
A rock in the desert
"where no one knows me,
just to
sit alone for a day."

His eyes gain hope when he says, "What about
a big ocean liner
a traveling school
to roam the seas
with specialists to teach farm workers about
the next destination—
wouldn't that be great!"

The ashram-like community vision—
he tried that twice: Forty Acres, La Paz
but still he hopes that one day...

"To see the face of God," that wish
so quiet I barely hear,
ask him to repeat,
can't believe he doesn't see it all around.
He insists, Catholic shiny-eyed boy,
if he is just good enough,
he will see that face one day.

FETCHING JUANA
December 18, 1991

The chapel at Our Lady of Guadalupe is full
of flowers on the stairs to the altar
of priests who have been 'round César for decades
of family and a few friends.
We come to say *Adiós* to Juana Chávez.

More personal than her husband's service
where César's *amigo* ex-Governor Jerry Brown
the media
even fired staff came,
César and Helen's children stumble on tears
find their way with words.
Then César reads telegram after telegram
from movie stars, singers and other celebrities
as if to assure us
himself
that his spotlight has not been extinguished.

I listen
to my heart
remembering
Juana's cackling laugh
the morning she showed me how to make tortillas
her busy bony fingers patting the *masa* into a ball
as she said something in Spanish I didn't get
as she put the ball down for another try.
Round tortillas hadn't been part of my day
only square ones
which didn't matter because
my husband and I were at-home that morning
in a simple house in San Jose
decorated with the warmth of Juana and Librado

and their son, their famous son,
whose life seemed an extension of theirs—
their lives not changed a bit—
their son's effect on other people not unexpected.

I know
from the way César responded to each phone call
those times Juana went into Good Samaritan
that the cord was never cut
between this woman and her son.
That's not to say he is a Mama's boy
only that he lives the life he does because she
brought hobos home to dinner
used *manzanillo* tea instead of prescriptions
            never forgot
            to talk every day
                        with her Maker.

Later, at the cemetery
waiting with friends near the gaping hole
I remember Juana's little bird-like "Aye, aye, aye"
as she mourned the lowering of her lifelong partner's casket
years before.

Suddenly
my friend Daneen elbows me,
points to swallows
approaching from our left.
Soaring like the Blue Angels
they reach the hole that awaits Juana
circle three times
and leave.
"They took her with them," my friend says.
And I watch them disappear
into thin blue sky.

THE UNSPEAKABLE LOSS OF FRED ROSS
San Francisco–October, 1992

Delancey Street courtyard.
Old friends swarming about
in spirited joyful reunion
layered over regret.
We've come
to tell Fred Ross goodbye.
Tall, lanky, proud man
gentle motivator
procurer of power.
Master organizer from World War II days
running Japanese relocation efforts
running Dust Bowl labor camps we read about
in John Steinbeck's books.
Then César's inspiration
and ours.
Fred's life, now his death
brings us back from disparate directions
to one purpose.

Inside the big room
where the memorial is to be held
I see César shaking hands
wooden
unfamiliar.
Never a good time to approach
I think I'll wait 'til after the service
to talk with him.

Eulogists reminisce.
The rich past
draws tears and laughter from the
gathered hundreds, then

it's César's turn.
Someone introduces him saying
he has laryngitis.
Diminished with grief,
he unfolds an old letter from Fred
as if it were disintegrating silk
reads Fred's words in
gravel voice.
Minutes click away in words sounding
like a piano without all its keys.
César says this is the most important letter
he ever received from Fred, yet
why?
The why is eclipsed
as the words trip over César's sorrow.
I do not like seeing his strength disabled,
his loss literally choking him.

Then I remember the time before this,
his mother's funeral,
at lunch in a room buoyant with sounds
of family and friends,
of tunes from a band Luis Valdez brought;
César sat apart that afternoon
not unlike the first time I saw him
thirty years earlier.

This is what the man does
drives to a private heart space,
for the moment at least,

a place to consider things
he believes no one else would understand.

The last story told, the last prayer offered
I follow my former boss, my old friend outdoors
watch him in a protective circle of men
rush across the courtyard
disappear up stairs into a room,
disappear from my sight for the last time
without a word.

To one of my departing friends I flip,
"Next time we're all together
it'll probably be for César's funeral"
thinking of some date a decade away
instead of five months.

part six

AFTER HE'S GONE

Truth and roses surround themselves with thorns.

Henry David Thoreau,
philosopher and writer

REMEMBERING CÉSAR ESTRADA CHÁVEZ
April 22, 1993

I did not think
you would go so soon
although surely your body
received mixed messages—
diligent diets,
repeated, debilitating fasts,
hikes up the mountain,
your fall off the porch a year or two before.

No tears come.
Perhaps because I am
so happy
to have known you
to have loved you
shared the good you brought
to thousands of people you knew
and didn't know.

Kaleidoscopic memories
tumble in patterns—
the times
I overheard you
counsel children,
unhappy spouses,
frustrated workers.
The time I felt the warmth of
your healing hand
on my sore back.

Yes, I remember the sting
of your disapproval
but what keeps resurfacing is your question,
a weedy thought in a swirl of dancers

during that party in the La Paz kitchen:
"Why do you like me?"
I shall always remember
that the powerful
and the powerless
need to know
they are liked
and why.

So let me tell you now.
It was your passion for *life*
not just the union—
that transformed us.
You took us with you
on a roller-coaster ride
I wouldn't have missed
for anything.

Vaya con Dios, César. ¿Tienen los angelitos una unión?

A FUGUE OF ROSES

I.   Like Beethoven's Dundundun-dah. Dundundun-dah...
or threads woven through a good novel
roses were our fugue, and
the more I think of it,
their thorny beauty perfectly
described the way we were with each other.

The first time you mentioned roses to me,
you asked serious as a doctor instructing a new mother—
"You know how to prune roses? You must be very careful to..."
That was my first year in Delano, 1968.

II.   The next time was at La Paz, 1972.
With tongues whose thorniness stung
as much as any rose,
we had punctured one another's thin skin
just before you'd left on a trip
to a boycott city in the East.
When you returned,
you brought, from the airplane,
two little single-shot brown heart-shaped bottles
Paul Masson Rare Cream Sherry vessels
and put them on the corner of my desk.
Then you took one back.
"We can keep roses in these—
one on your desk, one on mine."

Every few mornings
I stopped by the rose garden
out front of the Admin Building
to pick a fresh bud.
Sometimes you'd gotten there first,
flicking aphids off
pruning.

One afternoon
I reached across your desk
to empty the little sherry bottle
of the droopy yellow bud—
it never blossomed.
But you put your hand out to stop me.
"I'm talking to it," you said.
You didn't laugh so I swallowed mine.

What were you telling the rose?
That you thought she was beautiful?
That you were scared
about the contract on your life—
knowing the three shifts of hulking guards
wouldn't stop a bullet?
Did you confess to the rose
your fury that
the Giumarras' bank account was bigger than yours,
so how could you fund the strike at their ranch?
Did you speak to the thirsty petals
of frustration
over all that you had to do
or
of joy—a new grandchild?

Watching you I wondered
How much you have changed
from the runt in *pachuco* clothes.

III.   After two years of roses from your garden, I left
to tend my own landscape.

The first time you visited me
in the house I bought all my own,
you said, "Too bad there aren't any roses here."

I led you out behind the bamboo fence,
to six roses bushes I'd rescued
from someone replacing them with Astroturf.
You bent to
sniff the Tropicana and then,
reaching into the front pocket of your chinos,
asked, "May I?"
I saw the pen knife
hesitated to let you cut the bud,
but once again unable to tell you No, said
"Sure."

Carefully, carefully,
just above the V where a new leaf climbed up the stem,
you slit the flower
handed it to me.

IV.   Our fugue's finale—1985.
I was housesitting.
You tracked me down and
when I answered the doorbell,
there you stood on the bottom step
looking up at me
schoolboy-sweet bashful
without a word
handed me a rose
a yellow bud
from your mother's *jardin*.

V.   Now, 1993,
in a pine box Richard built,
you lie in the plot at La Paz
where we used to snip unfolding blossoms,
you lie in the bed of roses
forever.

LEGACY

I.   One year from the day César passed
his friends and admirers flocked to Sacramento—
some walking the whole way from Delano
again.
One man slumped in a wheelchair
bearing a sign saying he'd walked the first time
nearly three decades before
the whole way;
this time someone pushed his wheelchair
the whole three hundred-some miles.

I hunted through the throngs
for familiar faces
leapt at each rare chance to say,
"Remember the first march?"

Then on a quiet patch of lawn
I bathed in joyous shouts
Viva La Causa, Viva César Chávez.
The persevering sounds,
the sight of *esperanza* and *dignidad*
etched in the faces around me
was enough to erase the sad old man picture
of my last encounter with this crowd's hero,
enough to wipe out doubts about
the union's future.
I filled my thoughts with flashing images
of César speaking at a Democratic Party Convention
of César on picket lines, facing off with filthy-mouthed growers
of César standing on his head doing yoga—
he came a long way from that runt in *pachuco* clothes.
On and on thoughts tumble
until they are swallowed up in the

140

revelry of thousands upon thousands
of spirited workers around me.
As the slogan on the sunny-gold t-shirt I bought that day says,
"Cada trabajador es un organizador"—
"Each worker is an organizer." No more waiting
for César, one man, to do the job.

II.   August, 1994
President Bill Clinton awards
the Presidential Medal of Freedom
to Helen
saying, "César was
one of the most influential labor leaders of this century."

III.   By the end of 1994,
farm workers organize unions
in Bolivia, Chile, Mexico, and Canada.
From Hayward and Fresno, California to
Flint and Lansing, Michigan,
streets are renamed for the undaunted leader.
San Jose, where he caught the organizing bug,
labels a popular park and school César Estrada Chávez.

IV.   Stevie Wonder
Lalo Guerrero
Agustin Lira
serenade the valiant one.

V.   A mural with César's face appears in a Hollywood movie
—*La Familia* I think
shown in *los barrios* and the suburbs
because since the March to Sacramento
Latinos can walk more proudly
in once forbidden streets.

VI. Barrios Unidos opens
the César Chávez Institute
for Social Change
at the University of Santa Cruz.
In Fresno something like the institute is shepherded
by a man from Gandhi's India.
And in far-away Yemen,
the father of Nagi Daifullah,
the young farm worker killed by the cop in the Seventies,
says he is raising funds to build a temple
to honor his son and
César Chávez.

VII. In 1995
a few brave farm workers march
five-abreast with unionists, consumers, clergy
through the streets of Watsonville, California
showing support for strawberry harvesters
the UFW hope to sign up as members.
So many *freseros* already fired
because they'd joined.
Fear, doubt, questioning eyes line the sidewalks.
In this big crowd,
the most beautiful sight of all
dozens and dozens of Teamsters—
a miracle of renewed realization that
a house divided cannot withstand corporate greed.

VIII. A young man
who shook César's hand once
admired him many times,
on the first anniversary
of César's death,
says it best:
"César was
a touchable hero."

M O V E M E N T ' S   20TH   A N N I V E R S A R Y

Daneen Montoya, César Chávez, Susan Drake
San Jose, California
1982

Photographer unknown

CÉSAR

*Armando Garcia and
the Reverend Eugene Boyle
circa 1980*

© *Susan Samuels Drake*

CÉSAR AND JUANA

A YEAR AFTER CÉSAR DIED

Governor Pete Wilson objected to a proposal
that César's birthday become a state holiday.

April 1994

© *Paul Duginski*

FACE-LIFT

Some women at 60
attempt to surgically sustain their youth
as if to preserve their very souls.
I never banked on looks,
yet seeing my good fortune in the mirror,
cannot send bouquets only to ancestors.
Because knowing César,
being welcomed into farm workers' lives
supplied something less expensive than collagen,
less bruising than a plastic surgeon's knife.

I know,
we all know, don't we,
that we come equipped with Self.
Blossom or wither—
a lot depends on who we hang around with.
César turned up the light in my eyes
girded my native determination and trust
that everyone can change,
situations can change
and be changed.

He dared to step off the beaten path
persevered when thorns and stones
obstructed his course,
was unafraid of offending if the cause was right.
His sit-down-and-read-about-it search for answers
never flagged.

He believed in my writing, my graces, my spunk.
And when he turned away from me
I found my own path,
so that when he came back
I didn't lose my way.

No one taught me better than he—
either by example or in reaction to him—
that forgiveness is a must.
That is why I agree with the young man who said,
"César is a touchable hero."
Because his life touched mine,
it is easy for me to look in the mirror
and I am
but one of millions.

NOTES

If you want to learn more historical details, I recommend *Fight in the Fields* (Harcourt Brace, 1997) by Susan Ferriss and Ricardo Sandoval.

ALRA, Agricultural Labor Relations Act (1975): Under Governor Jerry Brown's administration, César and others convinced the governor this act would protect rights of workers in agriculture. Unfortunately, as governors change, their appointments reflect their politics. For the most part, the workers have experienced years, even decades, of stalls by the board this act set up to protect their interests.

Chávez, Helen: César's wife

Chávez, Juana: César's mother

Chávez, Richard: César's brother, a carpenter and the most active movement member of César's five siblings. Directed the New York Grape Boycott, the Farm Workers Service Center, the construction of buildings at The Forty Acres and the barbecuing for staff parties. César called him "Rookie."

Coffield, Father John: A Roman Catholic priest from a Southern California parish, donated free time to working with the union.

Day, Mark: Franciscan priest who worked solely with the farm workers' movement. He left the union and the priesthood and currently produces documentaries on the downtrodden and rebellious.

Drake, Jim: My husband from 1959-1973. His letter to my parents refers to his schooling, which was at Occidental College, Los Angeles, California and Union Theological Seminary, New York City. He currently is a community organizer for the Industrial Areas Foundation, founded by Saul Alinsky whose theories gave birth to the Community Service Organization for which César, Dolores Huerta and Gilbert Padilla first worked.

El Malcriado: Newspaper of news articles, features and cartoons relating to this farm workers' movement.

El Teatro Campesino (The Farmworker Theater): Luis Valdez and Agustín Lira combined hilarity, caricature and pathos to relieve tensions and embolden workers to carry on with their struggle.

Friel, Mary Jean: A Roman Catholic sister assisting César in the office in 1973.

Gomez, José: César's other administrative assistant in 1973.

Giumarra (John Sr. and Jr.): The Giumarra family owned the largest acreage of table grapes in the Delano area during the 1960s and 1970s. Father and son presented opposition to the unionization of their hundreds of workers.

Hartmire, Chris: Director of the California Migrant Ministry, later now known as the National Farm Worker Ministry. He was Jim's and my boss, although he didn't contradict any plans César had for our work.

Huerta, Dolores: Vice President of the United Farm Workers, fierce negotiator during the grape strike, leader in the American Women's Movement.

Lira, Agustín: Collaborator in *El Teatro Campesino*. Composer and singer of original music reminiscent of traditional Mexican music as well as inspired modern work that reminds listeners of the culture that deserves preservation.

Migrant Ministry, California: A branch of the National Council of Churches that, historically, ministered to agricultural field workers with Bible studies and games to entertain the children in the migrant camps. In the early 1960s, Chris Hartmire was directed to take a more active approach in helping the workers gain political strength and improvements in the economics and safety of their work.

National Labor Relations Act/Board: The Act was written to protect American laborers and govern their working conditions but omitted farm workers.

Ohta, Kerry: Worked out César's astrological chart.

Proposition 22: In California, proposed an Act to create a five-person board, appointed by the governor, to call for secret ballot elections, which UFW supported, but would ban boycotts and strikes, the UFW's nonviolent tools (back-up methods to ensure contract negotiation) following successful elections. Later, the California Agricultural Labor Relations Act went on the books with a procedure intended to be fairer to growers and workers.

Rojas, Al: Had been an enemy Teamster member before working for the UFW as Field Office Director and then César's Administrative Assistant.

Valdez, Luis: International award-winning stage- and screenwriter, director and producer; *Zootsuit*, *La Bamba*, *Cisco Kid* and upcoming César Chávez story. Actor. Originator of *El Teatro Campesino*.

Ybarra, Mike: Initially a boycott volunteer, later César's driver and guard.

about the author

Susan Samuels Drake, a fourth-generation Californian, began working with César Chávez in 1962. Susan worked in the Farm Workers Credit Union and the UFW's legal department, while her husband, Jim Drake, became Chávez' first Administrative Assistant and later headed the union's boycott department and organizing department. In 1971 she became César's secretary.

Susan Drake's nostalgic pieces and humorous essays have won awards from newspapers and literary magazines. She is a member of the National Writers Union.

This collection of poetry distills a full-length, as yet unpublished memoir of her years with the farm workers' movement.

c o l o p h o n

Offset printed by Kate Hitt at Many Names Press.
Please address inquiries to:
Post Office Box 1038
Capitola, California, 95010
Telephone: 831-475-5863

4-color and black and white scans and film output were done
at Prism Photographics in Santa Cruz, California.

Annie Browning set the type in Galliard roman, italic and bold
with accents set in Avenir.

Graciela Hernandez composed the cover design.

This edition of 2,000 copies was printed on Fraser Worx 60# text,
recycled and acid-free, using soy-based inks. 100 additional
books with digitally copied text were made at DeHart's in
Santa Clara, California.